THE ORIGIN OF LIFE ON EARTH

AN AFRICAN CREATION MYTH

Retold by David A. Anderson/SANKOFA   Illustrated by Kathleen Atkins Wilson   Designed by Pete Traynor

SIGHTS PRODUCTIONS   MT. AIRY, MD.

INTRODUCTION

THE PLANET ON WHICH WE LIVE TODAY once had but few people. Those early people must have found the world both frightening and marvelous. There were forest fires and floods, erupting volcanos and electrical storms, and many other forces of which they had no understanding. But the *great* mystery was the question of life itself. The people wanted to know:

How did life get into the body in the first place?

Where is life when it is not in the body of a person or an animal?

The early people looked at the stars and the sun, and the moon in all its phases. They listened to animals grunting, growling, whimpering, crying, and they compared all of it to the way people spoke. Animals dug, scratched and clawed; but people lifted, tossed, caught, pointed and drew signs in the dirt. The people dreamed and the people imagined, and they brought forth answers to some of the things that worried them.

Now at that time people lived in small groups, and the groups lived apart from each other. It would be this way for thousands of years. But about 1,000 years ago, people living in villages scattered west and north of the Niger (ny-jer) River delta, began to look for opportunities to come together. They bought goods from each other, and they sold goods to each other. The more often they did this, the more they were able to see that they had common interests. Villages began to band together into towns. The desire to band together brought on the desire to talk to each other about the questions that had always worried people. More

and more they were able to share what each imagined or believed to be good answers. Much of what they shared was woven into cloth; carved into wood and ivory, cast into bronze, brass and gold; expressed in song and dance. Tools, clothes, furniture and houses were made more pleasing by the work of the artists among the people.

The people's appreciation for what they had done and what they *could* do became sacred; it became part of the Yoruba religion. It had taken a long time but the people who created these towns and cities and artwork, were sharing in so many ways that they called themselves Yoruba (yah-roo-bah).

In Yoruba religion, Olorun (oh-loe-roon) is God-Almighty. Olorun lives in the sky with many assistants or agents, called orishas (oh-ree-shahs). THE ORIGIN OF LIFE ON EARTH is the story of how orisha Obatala (oh-bah-tah-lah) was sent by Olorun to make Earth and the first people.

This creation myth comes to us from the distant past. As teller of myth, I peer into the mystery of what long-ago people did to explain the world to themselves. I see their humanness. I tell their sacred story as fact.

Is this story true? Well, the forebears told it to me through my father, who got it from his mother. She got it from my father's grandmother, who got it from her father, who was *that-there* African. So it was *that-there* African who gave it to me as I have given it to you.

David A. Anderson/SANKOFA

Now the Yoruba say that long before there were people, all life was in the sky. Olorun lived there with many orishas, both male and female. Olorun understood both male and female orishas; yet Olorun was more than male and female. To be sure, each orisha had powers, but Olorun was *all-powerful*. Olorun was supreme.

Everything the orishas needed was in the sky and close by the young baobab tree. Olorun called the orishas to that tree. They came in fine clothes and jewelry made of gold. Olorun told them: "The sky stretches in all directions and far beyond this baobab tree. The sky, and even beyond the sky, is yours to explore." But everything the orishas *wanted* was close by the baobab tree; and all the orishas, save one, were content.

Obatala was the orisha that was not content. He wanted to put his powers to use. He often gazed out into space thinking, wondering. He spent even more time peering down, into and through the mists that swirled beneath the sky kingdom. Thinking. Wondering. He studied the area beneath the mists, and came to understand that far below, was empty, endless water.

Obatala told Olorun how troubled he was: "Here in the sky we orishas have everything we need. We even have powers, but there is never a need to use these powers. Yet below the mists there is only a watery waste. If there was something firm upon the water, then we could create a world and beings to take care of that world. Such beings would need our help; we could use our powers to help them."

Olorun was moved by Obatala's concern, and said, "Very well then. Prepare yourself for I am sending you down to the watery wastes to begin the work."

So Obatala went to Orunmila, the orisha with the power to see into the future. Obatala said, "The one who is supreme over everything has told me to go down below the mists and create a place where life can take root and bloom. Please tell me what I must do to get ready for this task."

Orunmila agreed. He uncovered his divining tray and sprinkled it with a powder that was made of baobab roots. Onto it he cast 16 palm kernels. After the nuts rolled to a stop, Orunmila studied the marks they had made in the powder. He gathered up the palm kernels and cast them again. He studied the new marks. He cast the palm kernels again. Orunmila began to see trails and patterns and he studied these, too. In all, he cast the palm kernels eight times, and he read the meanings each time. At last he said to Obatala, "You will need a chain of gold to stretch from here to there. Gather up all the sand you can find in the sky. Take palm nuts and maize too. Also take *the egg:* it contains the personalities of all the other orishas, both male and female."

Obatala thanked Orunmila. He then went to each orisha and he asked them for their gold. Both male and female gave him everything they had that was made of gold. These he gave to the goldsmith, who melted them down and began to forge the melted gold into links.

While the goldsmith worked, Obatala gathered the other things he would need. He scooped up all the sand he could find and placed it in a snail shell. To the sand he added a pinch of baobab powder. Not far from the baobab tree he found palm nuts, and maize, and other seed. He placed these, and the snail shell full of sand in his shoulder bag. But he wrapped *the egg* carefully in the cloth of his own clothing, then bound it to his chest where it would be warm.

The goldsmith showed the chain to Obatala who said, "But there must be a hook at one end." The goldsmith replied, "But I have used all the gold. There is no more gold!" Obatala said, "Nevertheless, make a hook for the chain. Use some of the links."

The goldsmith melted down some of the links and made a hook for the chain. Obatala was pleased, and with his bag hanging from his shoulder, he hooked the chain into the sky. Then, gripping the chain with his hands, he began lowering himself.